CLAIRE CLONINGER

POSTCARDS

For People in Love

This book is lovingly dedicated to
Virginia and Charlie deGravelles, my parents,
and to the memory of
Marjie and Dobbin Cloninger, my parents-in-law,
in whose lives I have seen love lived out,

and to my husband, Spike,
who has made our marriage a refuge and an adventure.

CLAIRE CLONINGER

POSTCARDS

For People in Love

WORD PUBLISHING
Dallas•London•Vancouver•Melbourne

POSTCARDS FOR PEOPLE IN LOVE

Unless otherwise indicated, Scripture quotations used in this book are from
The Holy Bible, New Century Version, copyright © 1987, 1988, 1991 by Word Publishing, Dallas, Texas 75039.

**Published in association with the literary agency of Alive Communications,
P.O. Box 49068, Colorado Springs, Colorado, 80949.**

Library of Congress Cataloging-in-Publication Data:
Cloninger, Claire.
    Postcards for people in love / Claire Cloninger.
        p.   cm.
    ISBN 0-8499-1208-3
        1. Married people—Religious life. 2. Unmarried couples—
Religious life. 3. Love—Religious aspects—Christianity—
Meditations. 4. Imaginary letters. I. Title.
    BV4596.M3C58 1995
    242'.644—dc20

95-2866
CIP

Printed in the United States of America.
5 6 7 8 0 1 2 3 4 9 DKN 0 9 8 7 6 5 4 3 2 1

Contents

Introduction

I grew up in the shadow of a great love. My dad adored my mom, and she was totally committed to him. This September they will celebrate their sixtieth wedding anniversary. I was also blessed with a beautiful model of married love in the marriage of my husband's parents. Their hearts were so full of each other it showed in everything they did.

So it would seem that if love could be learned by osmosis or by imitation, my husband, Spike, and I would automatically have had a strong marriage. It didn't work like that. We had to build our own relationship a day at a time, and in the early years especially, we struggled. I remember some days when it felt a little like our love was hanging by a thread.

It was not until we began to go together, in faith, to God's Word for its guidelines and promises that our marriage really began to get a firm footing. It was that Word, grafted into our hearts by the Holy Spirit, that provided the solid rock we needed to build on.

When our son, Andy, and his precious Jenni said "I do" nearly three years ago, I knew that their way to a strong relationship would be less circuitous than ours simply because they were already on a journey of faith. As I've watched the prayerful and united way they've dealt with their daily difficulties, it has confirmed my belief that having God's Word at the center of two hearts is the surest way to make them one.

This book has grown out of my desire to show the incredible relevance of God's ageless, timeless wisdom to modern marriages. Each "postcard" is taken from one or more verses of Scripture about love, and each contains a personal, present-tense message of guidance, hope, or healing for couples who long to deepen their love for one another. It is my prayer that these little postcards from the heart of the Father will open the spirits of many people to God's power and strengthen the bonds of many marriages with his love.

Claire

Your Marriage Is a Gift

So the LORD God caused the man to sleep very deeply, and while he was asleep, God removed one of the man's ribs. Then God closed up the man's skin at the place where he took the rib. The LORD God used the rib from the man to make a woman, and then he brought the woman to the man.

And the man said,

"Now, this is someone whose bones came from my bones,
    whose body came from my body.
I will call her 'woman,'
    because she was taken out of man."

So a man will leave his father and mother and be united with his wife, and the two will become one body.

The man and his wife were naked, but they were not ashamed.

GENESIS 2:21–25

So God created human beings in his image. . . . He created them male and female. God looked at everything he had made, and it was very good.

GENESIS 1:27, 31a

My dear children,

*Y*our marriage is a gift, and each of you is a gift to the other. Do not treat this matter lightly, for I deem it highly important. When I made human beings, male and female, they were the pride and joy of my creation. When I looked at what I had made, how proud I was! I knew right then that what I had created was very good. The two of you were joined in my sight to be companions on your journey through life. To comfort and to love one another. To leave behind your family of origin and become a whole new entity—one, that once existed as two. Continue to give yourselves to one another as a sacred gift. There is to be no shame between you, my precious children. Your bodies are beautiful. They were created for you to share and celebrate. Your minds are amazing. They were designed so that you could think and create and share intimate moments of communication with one another. Your spirits are unique. They were designed to know me and give me glory. So enter in with gladness. Every day bring fresh hope and high expectations to this adventure known as love!

Your Creator,
God

Don't Miss My Meaning

. . . *These three things continue forever: faith, hope, and love. And the greatest of these is love.*

1 CORINTHIANS 13:13

My dear child,

The most important word in any language is the word **love**. But its truest meaning has been blended with this and that until it's very much diluted. Think about it. You wouldn't find it the least bit unusual to hear phrases like "I love chocolate" or "I love to ski." So it might be easy for you to miss the depth of my meaning when I tell you to love each other. What **is** my meaning? I'm not speaking of a slight preference or a sentimental feeling. The love of which I speak is a commitment, a choice to live in a top-priority relationship with another. It is a decision to serve and encourage and bless the one you love, helping your mate reach his or her full potential and attain his or her highest aspiration. Love means loyalty, sacrifice, and endurance. But it also means shared laughter and deep joy. Love is strong. Strong enough to overcome obstacles and change lives. But love is also vulnerable. Vulnerable enough to show weakness, to confess sin, and to ask for help. Without love the world can be a bleak and lonely planet. But with love, there is meaning, purpose, and great beauty. Love requires the best of everything I've put in you. And love fulfills the highest purpose for which you were created.

My child, I am calling you to love,
God

I Await Your Invitation

Human life comes from human parents, but spiritual life comes from the Spirit.
JOHN 3:6

I tell you the truth, whoever hears what I say and believes in the One who sent me has eternal life. That person will not be judged guilty but has already left death and entered life.
JOHN 5:24

. . . I came to give life—life in all its fullness.
JOHN 10:10

Here I am! I stand at the door and knock. If you hear my voice and open the door, I will come in and eat with you and you will eat with me.
REVELATION 3:20

With God's power working in us, God can do much, much more than anything we can ask or imagine.
EPHESIANS 3:20

LORD, you have examined me
and know all about me.
You know when I sit down and when I get up.
You know my thoughts before I think them.
You made my whole being;
you formed me in my mother's body.
PSALM 139:1–2, 13

My child,

I know you have many hopes for yourself and your loved one in this life you share together. I too have hopes for you, for I love you and desire good things for you—better things, in fact, than you can ask or even imagine! I want to give you abundant life. Life with a capital L! Not life that stays on the plain, hard surface of physical facts, but life that dives down deep, below the surface of physical reality into the rich, brilliant colors of my spiritual depths. Though you have not always been aware of my presence, I have known you at every phase in your life. I have known you since before your birth, when you were but a flickering light in my imagination, and I have loved you. But now it is time for you to know me, my child, for you will need my peace and my power. You will need my protection and my counsel as you embark on this exciting journey as man and wife. Do you know how close I am to you now? I stand outside the door of your heart, knocking. Will you invite me into the everyday realities of your life? Will you accept my Son as your Savior and my Spirit as your guide? As I dwell at the center of your being, I will forgive your sin, heal your wounds, and equip you for the journey.

I await your invitation,
God

Take Time for Each Other

Teach us how short our lives really are
so that we may be wise.

PSALM 90:12

There is a time to cry
and a time to laugh.
There is a time to be sad
and a time to dance.

ECCLESIASTES 3:4

Dear child,

*A*s you live out your life with the one you love, place a high priority on time together. Set aside special times to be alone with one another because time not spoken for will mysteriously disappear into the black hole of busyness. Plan a regular evening for just the two of you. Share a meal together. Sit across a table from each other and talk about the things you are going through. Share the deep feelings and the special concerns of your hearts. Learn to find fun and laugh together. And learn to cry together when sad times come. Take an occasional day off to walk along a beach, hike a mountain trail, or lie on a blanket under a tree together. Enjoy the beauty of my creation, and celebrate the fact that I created you for one another. After an afternoon or an evening spent together, you will return to your routine with spirits refreshed and love rekindled.

Take time to enjoy each other!
God

What a Way to Start the Day!

This is the day that the Lord has made.
Let us rejoice and be glad today!

PSALM 118:24

The Lord's love never ends;
his mercies never stop.
They are new every morning;
Lord, your loyalty is great.

LAMENTATIONS 3:22–23

Lord, every morning you hear my voice.
Every morning, I tell you what I need,
and I wait for your answer.

PSALM 5:3

Dearest child,

Every day when you wake up you have a choice. You can look at the day that stretches out before you and see it as an obstacle course built of problems and potential disappointments. Or you can see a day of joy and challenge—a day I desire to share with you. The difference this will make in your life is enormous! You will face the new day knowing that your own personal Guide is just waiting to steer you through your commitments and responsibilities, helping you at every turn. You will greet each morning knowing that you have a Friend and a Father to talk to all day long in that secret room in your heart where my Son and I have come to live. The difference this can make in your marriage is also enormous! You can set the mood for your household by your faith-filled and optimistic outlook. And if you will spend the first minutes of each day sharing your heart with me, soon the eyes of your spirit will be opened wide to see my mercies that are new every morning.

What a way to start the day!
God

I Will Fill the Rooms with Beauty

It takes knowledge to fill a home
with rare and beautiful treasures.

PROVERBS 24:4

Always be humble, gentle, and patient, accepting each other in love. You are joined together with peace through the Spirit, so make every effort to continue together in this way.

EPHESIANS 4:2–3

. . . Your beauty should come from within you—the beauty of a gentle and quiet spirit that will never be destroyed and is very precious to God.

1 PETER 3:4

Dear child of mine,

*D*o you desire to furnish your home with beautiful things, to make it as gracious and lovely as you possibly can? If you let me, I will help you fill the rooms with beauty that cannot be bought. In a world consumed with pride and arrogance, **humility** is a rare treasure. Give it a place of honor in your home, and you will see what loveliness it adds to all who live and visit there. In a world that pushes and shoves, threatens and bullies, **gentleness** is an adornment of unusual beauty. Let gentleness be displayed throughout your home in all that is done, and your lives will be enriched by its beauty. In a world of anxious striving and restless ambition, **patience** is a pearl of great price. Furnish the rooms of your home with patience, and observe what grace and charm it adds to your life. In short, my child, enjoy decorating your home. Buy what you can afford. Paint and polish, arrange and display your possessions with love and care. But remember: The most important furnishings in a home are the rare and precious qualities that only my Holy Spirit can provide.

Yours for a beautiful home,
God

You Were Made for Each Other

But in the Lord women are not independent of men, and men are not independent of women. This is true because woman came from man, but also man is born from woman. But everything comes from God.

1 CORINTHIANS 11:11–12

O, my beloved children,

I am writing now to all who are married. When I look back on Adam's delight in the creation of Eve, and Eve's delight in her strong new husband, I am saddened to see the cruelty and competition that creeps into marriages. This I never intended.

You wives, think about it. I created Eve by taking a rib from Adam's side. You are meant to be the completion of his skeleton—the thing that holds him up and keeps him together! He needs you beside him to respect him, affirm him, and treat him with kindness. When you belittle him or show a lack of faith in his ability, it's as though you pulled a rib out—something in him collapses.

You husbands, do you really think you have no need of women? What was the doorway through which you entered this world? You were issued into life itself through a woman, your mother! This wife you promised to love has much beauty to share with you. Do not crush her spirit by pulling away into your own cocoon. Talk to her. Listen to her. Invest your understanding in this woman's life, and your own life will be many times richer for it.

Oh, my children, don't you see? You were made for each other! Begin today to be what I designed you to be.

Your Father who loves you,
God

Weave My Love into Yours

So a man will leave his father and mother and be united with his wife, and the two will become one body.

GENESIS 2:24

A rope that is woven of three strings is hard to break.

ECCLESIASTES 4:12b

My dear children,

To be married is to enter a new realm of life. When you promised yourselves to each other, you left behind the room of childhood in which you were dependent upon your parents, and you stepped over the threshold into the room of adult love and commitment. It is within the bonds of this commitment that two distinctly different personalities are formed into one. This process takes years. It is like the weaving together of two distinctly different kinds of thread into a whole new cloth, a cloth with many functions. It is a tent, a covering from the hostile elements of the changing seasons. It is a colorful quilt that warms the two who share it. It is a sheer, gauzy curtain that offers privacy while allowing the sunlight to shine through. But the most beautiful and enduring marriage of all is not merely the weaving of two lives but of three, for woven into the strongest unions is the golden strand of my love that endures forever. May the cloth of your marriage be woven of three strands.

Lovingly,
God

Learn to Confess and Forgive

Most importantly, love each other deeply, because love will cause many sins to be forgiven.

1 PETER 4:8

Confess your sins to each other.

JAMES 5:16

Forgive us for our sins, just as we have forgiven those who sinned against us.

MATTHEW 6:12

My beloved child,

*Pay attention to me now. If you can **grasp** this message with your mind and then allow me to **graft** it into your heart, it will change the quality of your life. You know that there will inevitably be times in your marriage when you hurt or disappoint each other. That is why there is no way in this world to live harmoniously without the balancing virtues of confession and forgiveness. When you have wronged your loved one, don't waste a minute trying to justify yourself. Go immediately and confess your wrong. And when the tables are turned and you are the one wronged, don't waste time nursing your wounds or enjoying your martyrdom. Forgive your loved one then and there, and be reconciled. Confession and forgiveness will be like a seesaw tilting one way, then another, throughout your life together. Sometimes you will be the one who needs to confess and sometimes, the one who needs to forgive. Stay tender-hearted toward me, and I will give you a spiritual nudge when it's time for you to do one or the other. If you learn to use these two tools, you'll find that they will keep the quality of your love in good repair.*

Confess and forgive,
God

Stay Focused on Me

The thing you should want most is God's kingdom and doing what God wants. Then all these other things you need will be given to you.

MATTHEW 6:33

In all the work you are doing, work the best you can. Work as if you were doing it for the Lord, not for people.

COLOSSIANS 3:23

Dearest children,

*Do you feel fractured by all the confusion in your lives? Are you forced to think of, and plan, and do so many things that you feel like an array of puzzle pieces that won't hold together? Do you long for more time with each other and yet feel too tired to enjoy it? Let me open a window in your spirits so you can catch a new vision. Now pay attention. Much of the confusion in your lives is a result of focusing on too many things. Not necessarily **doing** too many, but **focusing** on too many. Focus on me. I will become the unifying center of your life together. Keep your inner gaze fixed on me, and I will knit your hearts together. Work as if I were your boss. Deal with the people in your day as if I were present in each interaction. (I am, you know!) Desire my ways and welcome my presence—in your home, your car, your office—and then watch your fractured lives come together. Stay focused on me,*

And I will give you peace,
God

Share Your Spiritual Food

Your promises are sweet to me,
sweeter than honey in my mouth!

PSALM 119:103

Always remember these commands I give you today. Teach them to your children, and talk about them when you sit at home and walk along the road, when you lie down and when you get up.

DEUTERONOMY 6:6–7

It is the Spirit that gives life. The flesh doesn't give life. The words I told you are spirit, and they give life.

JOHN 6:63

My child,

My words are health and life to you and your loved ones. They are like powerful spiritual food that nourishes and builds up the inner person. Don't compartmentalize your life, thinking that the things of the spirit are only for Sundays. Your spirit is hungry Monday through Saturday, too! For just as your physical body needs to be fed and nourished every day, so does your spirit. Yet many people in the world go through their lives starving for spiritual food because they have never come to know me and have never fed on my Word. Do not simply read these words of mine. Take them into your life. Chew on them. Digest them. Make them a part of you— your waking thought every morning and your silent prayer at night. Put them on the "menu" at every evening meal so your children can hear you discussing them and can develop a taste for them in their own lives. What more caring thing could you do for the ones you love than to share your spiritual food, helping them grow strong spiritually, wise beyond their years, and filled with an excitement and a zest for life?

Come and taste and see!
God

You Are Called to Sacrificial Loving

Wives, yield to your husbands, as you do to the Lord, because the husband is the head of the wife, as Christ is the head of the church. And he is the Savior of the body, which is the church. As the church yields to Christ, so you wives should yield to your husbands in everything.

Husbands, love your wives as Christ loved the church and gave himself for it to make it belong to God. Christ used the word to make the church clean by washing it with water. He died so that he could give the church to himself like a bride in all her beauty. He died so that the church could be pure and without fault, with no evil or sin or any other wrong thing in it. . . . The man who loves his wife loves himself. . . . But each one of you must love his wife as he loves himself, and a wife must respect her husband.

EPHESIANS 5:22–28, 33

My children,

Your marriage is of great value to me and to my kingdom. In fact, it should be a small, earthly picture of heaven's perfect love. If I could frame a picture of your marriage and hang it on my wall, what would I like to see in my picture frame? I would like to see the two of you living selflessly together in everyday ways, treasuring, respecting, and caring for each other. Both of you are called to sacrificial loving. As the church honors Christ, wives are to honor their husbands. And as Christ laid down his life for the church, husbands are to lay down their lives for their wives. Don't ever let your love dissolve into a squabble over "rights." Give even before it is asked of you. Give even more than is expected of you. Don't give only 50 percent; go all the way to 100 percent! If both of you will give like this, there will be enough love for each of you and an abundance of love left over. Love in this way, and your life together will bring great joy to you and great glory to me.

Begin today!
God

Love Is Not for the Hasty Heart

Love is patient and kind.

1 CORINTHIANS 13:4a

Be alert. Continue strong in the faith. Have courage, and be strong. Do everything in love.

1 CORINTHIANS 16:13–14

Precious child,

*L*ove is not for the hasty heart. It is not for the flighty, the frivolous, the faithless, or the fickle. Real love requires a strength and a steadiness that does not give up or give in. It means bearing with one another's flaws while celebrating one another's gifts. It means holding on through all the mountaintops and valleys of life, always forgiving the worst while believing in the best. Real love decorates the days with simple acts of kindness, small but thoughtful deeds that lift the spirit and light the dark corners of the soul. Are you wondering if you have what it takes to love with this much patience, to care with this much kindness? Apart from me, you will find many times it is not possible. But turn to me, my child, and I will build my patience into your character, and I will open a window of kindness in your heart.*

Let me fill you with real love,
God

My Wisdom Brings Balance

A person who does not have the Spirit does not accept the truths that come from the Spirit of God. That person thinks they are foolish and cannot understand them, because they can only be judged to be true by the Spirit. The spiritual person is able to judge all things . . .

1 CORINTHIANS 2:14–15

No one can serve two masters. The person will hate one master and love the other, or will follow one master and refuse to follow the other. You cannot serve both God and worldly riches.

MATTHEW 6:24

My children,

*M*any marriages have been sacrificed on the altar of materialism because neither husband nor wife had my spiritual perspective on financial matters. Perhaps you thought I had no opinions on a subject as worldly as finance. Quite the contrary! My Word contains more instruction on the subject of money than it does on the subject of prayer! Do you wonder why? It's simple, really. Nothing else in your earthly existence will compete more aggressively with me for first place in your heart than money.

Money will try to be your master. It will try to call the shots in your life. Money will try to crowd me and my principles out of your reasoning process, pushing me into a small corner of your life labeled **for Sundays only**. But my views on money are very relevant to everyday. They bring order and purpose to your financial goals and plans. They work to extricate you from the push and shove of competitive spending, and they release you into the joy of a balanced and grace-filled life. Don't be bullied by the frantic fiscal philosophy of this fallen world. Let my Spirit guide you into my wisdom . . .

And you will find peace,
God

I Have Wonderful Plans for You

Some of you say, "Today or tomorrow we will go to some city. We will stay there a year, do business, and make money." But you do not know what will happen tomorrow! Your life is like a mist. You can see it for a short time, but then it goes away. So you should say, "If the Lord wants, we will live and do this or that."

JAMES 4:13–15

. . . I know what I am planning for you, says the LORD. I have good plans for you, not plans to hurt you. I will give you hope and a good future.

JEREMIAH 29:11

My children,

As you make your plans together, don't get so deeply invested in your own agenda that you forget the part I wish to play in your lives. As you rush past me in the mornings on the way to carry out those plans you have made, don't you realize I am waiting here, hoping to hear from you, longing to guide you? You see, I have my own plans for you, my children. I have designed you for a wonderful purpose. And apart from me, you will never discover what it is. Living apart from me is like running the "machinery" of your lives without reading the owner's manual! Are you afraid that my plans for you will box you in or make you miserable? Don't you know how much I love you? These are plans to prosper you, to give you hope and a good future. Oh, my children, turn to me.

Let me show you my plans for you,
God

Build Your Family of Love

It takes wisdom to have a good family,
and it takes understanding to make it strong.

PROVERBS 24:3

Everyone who hears my words and obeys them is like a wise man who built his
house on rock. It rained hard, the floods came, and the winds blew and hit that house.
But it did not fall, because it was built on rock.

MATTHEW 7:24–25

Beloved child,

When you marry, even before you have children, you begin building something very precious to me—a family. Building a family is like building a house. When you build a house, first you level the land and lay a strong foundation for the house to rest upon. Next you raise the walls that will protect you from the world outside. You add windows to bring in light and fresh air. You put in doors to allow people to come and go. And finally, you put on a roof to provide a covering from the elements. If you are wise, my child, you will use the love and the strength and the mercy of my Son, Jesus, as building blocks for a strong family. He is the Rock of Ages, the firm foundation that cannot be shaken. He provides safe walls of protection from the outside world. He opens windows to bring in healing light and the refreshing breeze of his Holy Spirit. He is the open door of friendship that will make your home a welcome place for all who visit there. And he is the covering your family will need in the rough weather of life. Trust me, my child, and . . .

Build your house upon the Rock!
God

Love Speaks Softly

I may speak in different languages of people or even angels. But if I do not have love, I am only a noisy bell or a crashing cymbal.

1 CORINTHIANS 13:1

Dear child,

Have you heard the voice of love? Love speaks softly, gently, sometimes even silently. Love will not get into a shouting match with all the strident voices that compete for attention in this noisy world. Instead, it moves quietly among the needy, hearing the heart cry of the wounded and meeting needs without a lot of fanfare. Love is a good listener. It draws near to the one whose silent suffering never gets a hearing, and it picks up unspoken signals of distress. Love creates a climate where people of all ages feel safe to speak their minds, their hearts, and their deepest needs. Love slows down to be present to a child's questions, an old person's rambling remembrance, a teenager's frustration, a lover's sigh. Love says in a million silent ways, "You matter. I see what you're going through, and I care." It also says without any kind of sermon, "God loves you, and so do I." So, my child, let love be the silent song within your home today. Let it be the quiet message of hope you speak to your loved one. And as the two of you go through this busy day, let love be the message you bring to your hurting world. Without saying a word, you can speak in a language that only the heart can hear.

Speak love,
God

Trust the Process of "Becoming"

I do not mean that I am already as God wants me to be. I have not yet reached that goal but I continue trying to reach it and to make it mine. Christ wants me to do that, which is the reason he made me his.

PHILIPPIANS 3:12

Ask, and God will give to you. Search, and you will find. Knock, and the door will open for you. Yes, everyone who asks will receive. Everyone who searches will find. And everyone who knocks will have the door opened.

MATTHEW 7:7–8

My own dear child,

*When will you learn to be patient with yourself and your loved one? This life of love is a journey, not a destination. You are still traveling; you haven't arrived! So be gentle with your loved one and gentle with yourself as you travel together. You are someone "in process," someone "becoming." Trust this process. Let me explain. There is nothing wrong with a green apple. It is not wrong because it is not yet ripe and red. It is where it needs to be today in the ripening process. It is not yet complete, but it is becoming complete. The same applies to you. I'm still working in each of you to bring you to that place where my ultimate purposes can be fulfilled. But until I get you there, I want you to be my person in the everyday situations of your life **today**. As long as you are open to me, as long as you are asking, searching, knocking, and waiting for my answers, you're right where I want you. So love and accept each other where you are today. And . . .*

Find joy in the journey,
God

Tear Down Walls and Build Bridges

I will be in them and you will be in me so that they will be completely one. Then the world will know that you sent me and that you loved them just as much as you loved me.

JOHN 17:23

Where you go, I will go. Where you live I will live. Your people will be my people, and your God will be my God.

RUTH 1:16b

My dear children,

Soften your hearts toward one another. Allow my love to close the gap between you. Look at each other with eyes of love, seeing the beauty hidden there. See the invisible bond that exists between you, for you are surely one. Learn to care for the things your mate cares for. Learn to cherish the people your mate cherishes. Make a space in your heart for your partner's parents, grandparents, and siblings because when you married, you married more than an individual. You married a family! As a couple, try to find a way to share your faith in me. If there are differences in your beliefs, don't argue or fuss. (How senseless to use hateful words to prove a God of love!) Instead of arguing, listen with love. Try to understand each other. Then, on your knees, lift up to me whatever differences exist between you. Ask me to reveal my truth to both of you. Faith cannot be forced. I never forced it on you, did I? Love your partner; look for ways to tear down walls and build bridges between you. And most of all, pray for unity.

This is my desire for you,
God

I Am Your Security

[The LORD] will be your safety.
He is full of salvation, wisdom, and knowledge.
Respect for the LORD is the greatest treasure.

ISAIAH 33:6

A person who does what is right
and speaks what is right,
who refuses to take money unfairly . . .
who refuses to think about evil—
this is the kind of person who will be safe.
He will be protected as he would be in
a high, walled city.

ISAIAH 33:15–16

Dear child,

*L*ook around you. So many people in your frantic world are scrambling in all directions to buy security for themselves and their loved ones. They pour labor and money into a variety of schemes, seeking something to assure their safety as though this could somehow stem the inevitable tide of their own mortality. But the frail scaffolding they construct of investments, bank accounts, and insurance policies can only prop up a delusion of security for so long. Eventually, the fact must be faced by each man, each woman. There is no **lasting** security but my love. There is no **long-term** insurance but my grace. Compared to the eternal safety of a life lived in me, this world system, at best, offers only a diminished, impoverished, anemic imitation. Do you want security for yourself and your loved ones—security that reaches beyond life on planet earth? Put your life in right relation to me. Walk uprightly in your world and before me. Trust my promises, and live as my child.

I will be your everlasting security,
God

Make Your Home a Refuge

I will live an innocent life in my house.
I will not look at anything wicked.

Psalm 101:2–3

Do not change yourselves to be like the people of this world, but be changed within by a new way of thinking. Then you will be able to decide what God wants for you; you will know what is good and pleasing to him and what is perfect.

Romans 12:2

Dear child,

*Although you are surrounded on all sides by the morals and the madness of a sick society, your home can be a sanctuary of grace and peace. Determine to create for yourself and your loved ones an atmosphere of hope and harmony where people are valued, where friendships are nurtured, where my name is honored. Fill your home with all the joyous signs and sounds of life—flowers blooming, children laughing, a table spread with good things to eat. Make it a refuge, a safe place, where it is okay to be real and where it is acceptable to admit weakness—where prayer binds up the raveled edges of each day's disappointments. Take care to guard your home with all your might. Be selective about the words and thoughts you entertain there. Your television set often speaks with the accents of my enemy. It can bring the world's pollution into your living room, convincing you that there's no time for things that matter while you invest your precious hours in its mindless mumbling. Don't be molded to the world's insanity, my child, but let me mold you and your loved ones with the strong, calm sanity of **my** words.*

Your home is where my heart is,
God

You Can Find Harmony

Do you know where your fights and arguments come from? They come from the selfish desires that war within you. You want things, but you do not have them. . . . So you argue and fight. You do not get what you want, because you do not ask God. Or when you ask, you do not receive because the reason you ask is wrong. You want things so you can use them for your own pleasures.

So give yourselves completely to God. . . . You who are trying to follow God and the world at the same time, make your thinking pure.

JAMES 4:1–3, 7–8

My dear ones,

*Y*our lives together are to be like music—a beautiful harmony of two unique personalities combined. But creating this music is the work of a lifetime. It is a masterpiece that requires the best efforts of two committed people, for it is not easily achieved. Unfortunately, in many marriages, though both husband and wife desire harmony, it eludes them. It is thwarted by the discordant notes of selfishness in them that blare forth to spoil love's symphony. What are these discordant notes crying out for? Extravagant possessions. Selfish pleasures. Personal power. This is the music to which the world dances, the music that exalts the demigods of the common culture. Only as both of you yield to me, seeking my purposes and following my plans, will the sounds of selfishness cease and the music of two lives blend into one. The song of my heart will never harmonize with the raucous music of this world. For this reason, you will find you cannot dance with one foot in the world and one in the kingdom. Come to me, my children, and let me help you blend your lives into a lasting harmony.

We can make beautiful music together!
God

Do You Bear a Family Resemblance to Me?

Dear friends, we should love each other, because love comes from God. Everyone who loves has become God's child and knows God. Whoever does not love does not know God, because God is love.

1 JOHN 4:7–8

The Spirit we received does not make us slaves again to fear; it makes us children of God. With that Spirit we cry out, "Father." And the Spirit himself joins with our spirits to say we are God's children.

ROMANS 8:15–16

My child,

I have called you into my family, and that makes us kin. I am no longer only the God of whom you have heard and learned. I am now the One you know and believe in. Because you have invited me into your heart, you can call me "Father" as Jesus did. We are related in the closest way. Will people know this when they look at your life? Will they see in your eyes my graciousness, my gentleness, my love? Is there a family resemblance between us that others will recognize? The real test is not out in the public places where you use your best manners. The real test is in your own home with the ones who are closest to you. Do you bear a family resemblance to me in your own home? If someone who didn't know you could peep through the keyhole of your life, would they catch you in the act of being my child? Would they hear my gentleness in your voice and see my compassion in your eyes? Would they be able to see you forgiving, encouraging, and bringing joy to your family? The longer you know me, the more it should show.

Your loving Father,
God

Actions Speak Loudest

My children, we should love people not only with words and talk, but by our actions and true caring.

1 John 3:18

Do what God's teaching says; when you only listen and do nothing, you are fooling yourselves. Those who hear God's teaching and do nothing are like people who look at themselves in a mirror. They see their faces and then go away and quickly forget what they looked like. But the truly happy people are those who carefully study God's perfect law that makes people free, and they continue to study it. They do not forget what they heard, but they obey what God's teaching says. Those who do this will be made happy.

James 1:22–25

Dear child,

When it comes to love, anyone can "talk a good game." It is possible to say all the right words and never back them up with a single action. Sonnets and love songs may sound beautiful, but if they are only rhetoric, what real purpose do they serve? Beautiful but hollow words are little more than dry leaves carried off in the wind. Real love is lived out daily. It is a cool drink on a hot day, a cozy sweater in an autumn breeze, a home-cooked meal for a hungry stomach. Small and caring kindnesses are the evidence of love in action. Being there, listening, understanding, taking time to be together, choosing to forgive—these are ways of living out your commitment to care. And in an atmosphere of caring deeds, beautiful words of love ring true.

Actions speak loudest,
God

Love Has Good Manners

Love is not rude, is not selfish, and does not get upset with others.

1 Corinthians 13:5a

Lord, help me control my tongue;
help me be careful about what I say.

Psalm 141:3

Dear child of mine,

*W*hen you first learned to share your toys, to take turns, to say "please" and "thank you," you were learning the rudiments of loving behavior, for love has good manners. But unlike the child who sometimes learns to do these things mechanically without quite understanding why, I'm asking you to go deeper. I'm asking you to look behind the polite behavior and get in touch with the heart attitude. People with a loving heart attitude don't have to fake gracious behavior, for they genuinely value others. How do they do it? They have learned to see other people as I do, as precious children of mine. And they know when they look into the eyes of a friend or a stranger they are looking at a person for whom Jesus died. Seeing every person in this light ignites a desire to affirm rather than to negate, to bless rather than to belittle. And you will find, my child, that in blessing someone else you are also feeding the spring of hidden blessings that bubble up within your own heart!

Let yours be a loving heart,
God

Practice Being a Friend

By helping each other with your troubles, you truly obey the law of Christ.

GALATIANS 6:2

Two people are better than one . . .
If one falls down,
  the other can help him up.

ECCLESIASTES 4:9–10

In this world you will have trouble, but be brave! I have defeated the world.

JOHN 16:33

Dearest child,

*Y*ou are not to be a fair-weather friend to your loved one, for this love you share is "for better or for worse." When it comes to trouble, my child, no one is exempt. Everyone will have sorrowful seasons and difficult days. It's fairly easy for you to be sweet-natured and supportive when things are going well. But the true test of a marriage will come in the tough times. Sometimes one of you will be struggling while the other is at peace. The next time, the roles may be reversed. That is why the two of you must learn to share your trouble just as you share your joy. You must learn the meaning of being one so you can weather the storms together. Be ready to share your heart, to express your need. Be ready to listen and react with compassion. Practice being a friend as well as a lover. And in the midst of trials and troubles, remember, my child, you are already on the winning side. For Jesus walked this way before you, and he has defeated the darkness of the world!

Victoriously,
God

Celebrate Each Small Success

Love does not count up wrongs that have been done. Love is not happy with evil but is happy with the truth.

1 CORINTHIANS 13:5b–6

Show mercy, just as your Father shows mercy.

LUKE 6:36

Dearest child,

*H*ave you found yourself so much at odds with the one you love that you are adding up every mistake and flaw, keeping score on every blunder and sin? If you keep this up, it can become an addictive habit, and you'll find yourself inwardly smug and delighted every time you have another black mark to put against your loved one's name. Now I ask you, is that any way to love? Do I love you that way? Suppose I had been keeping that kind of score book on you your whole life long. Suppose you knew I was sitting up here in heaven with my pencil sharpened waiting for you to make another mistake! Wouldn't that make you all the more likely to fail? Instead, I forgive whatever you confess, and I give you a clean slate to work on. That's because I love you, and I long to see you succeed. I am just waiting to rejoice over your victories. Could you begin today to love like this—praying daily for the little victories, celebrating each small success? If you do, you'll discover that this kind of love is rich soil in which your loved one can grow better and stronger.

Try it and see!
God

I Have Designed a Home for You

My people will live in peaceful places
and in safe homes
and in calm places of rest.

Isaiah 32:18

My precious child,

The home I have designed for you to live in is filled with mercy and built of love. There is a welcome mat at the front door and a cozy fire burning in the fireplace on cold, winter evenings. Bright, fragrant flowers adorn the tabletops, and lovely paintings grace the walls. And throughout all the rooms of this home, there is the sweet aroma of peace. Here people are valued and accepted right where they are. Each one is seen as unique and is never compared to another. Each person's gifts are affirmed as special, and one is never held in more esteem than another. Approval comes to all who live here, no strings attached. Affirmation is not withheld until a certain level of performance is reached; nor is it given out like a prize in a contest. It is given freely with love. There is room to grow in this home I have for you. Room to grow emotionally and spiritually. Room to grow in the ability to give and receive, to love and believe. And in this home the sweet flower of forgiveness blooms year-round. Are you ready to move in, my child? My love is the key.

Welcome home!
God

Stand Firm in This Covenant

Marriage should be honored by everyone, and husband and wife should keep their marriage pure. God will judge as guilty those who take part in sexual sin.

HEBREWS 13:4

The only temptation that has come to you is that which everyone has. But you can trust God, who will not permit you to be tempted more than you can stand. But when you are tempted, he will also give you a way to escape so that you will be able to stand it.

1 CORINTHIANS 10:13

Child of mine,

You have made a serious commitment to love for a lifetime. But the society in which you live no longer views such a commitment as binding. In the world's eyes, marriages are no longer "'til death do us part" but "'til one of us decides it's not working out." Don't let that confound or confuse you. This is not the first time the world and I have disagreed! Listen, my child. I want you to stand firm in this covenant, just as you promised—for better or for worse, for richer or for poorer. And though you see all kinds of relationships and all kinds of behavior out there, hold your ground. You need not concern yourself with the immorality of others. I am speaking to you now. I want the two of you to keep yourselves for each other only. Just as the man who invests all of his money on the strongest stock gets the biggest return, you will reap the greatest personal benefit if you invest all of your love in the one relationship you've committed your all to. I'm aware that you may be tempted at times to be unfaithful. Look to me in those times, and I will give you an escape route. I promise. Hold tight to each other, my child, and . . .

Keep your eyes on me,
God

Put Fear Far from You

Where God's love is, there is no fear, because God's perfect love drives out fear.

1 JOHN 4:18a

She does her work with energy. . . .
She does not worry. . . .
      She looks forward to the future with joy.

PROVERBS 31:17a, 21a, 25b

Dearest child,

You have much to bring to this life of love. Bring your energy and your willingness to work hard. Bring your hope, your optimism, your faith in me. These qualities you will need every day in the ebb and flow of life's circumstances. But do not bring fear. Put it far from you, for fear can only paralyze love. It is a subtle captor that slips into your life and shackles your heart. You must break through its chains if you are to live in love. Call on me, my child, when you feel the pressure of fear around your heart, for my love can and will break through. Then, like a bird let out of a cage, your heart will soar up on faith into a future it has not yet seen, joyful in the knowledge that the days and hours and moments yet to be are held in the same merciful hands that hold today. That is when you will . . .

Look to the future with joy,
God

Can You Love As He Loved?

This is my command: Love each other as I have loved you. The greatest love a person can show is to die for his friends.

JOHN 15:12–13

This is how we know what real love is: Jesus gave his life for us. So we should give our lives for our brothers and sisters.

1 JOHN 3:16

Dear child,

What do you think of when you think of falling in love? Many people picture all the meaning and fulfillment their loved one will bring into their lives. But the truest picture of love is not painted in colors of what is to be gained but in colors of what is to be given. For love is an action word that depicts a life laid down. That's the kind of love Jesus is talking about when he calls us to love as He loves. The fullest measure of his love was this: He died for his friends. Are you prepared to love like this? Oh, I realize you may never be called to die a physical death for the one you love. But there are many ways of dying and many small deaths on the road to real love— everything from petty inconvenience to severe self-sacrifice. Are you prepared to die to your selfishness, your rights, your sometimes-stubborn determination to have everything go your way? Are you prepared to be spent and poured out on the altar of love? By the Spirit life of Jesus dwelling in you, it is possible to walk through the fire of dying to self and find the freedom of sacrificial love.

Trust my Holy Spirit,
God

To Grow Love, Plant Kindness

Do not be fooled: You cannot cheat God. People harvest only what they plant. If they plant to satisfy their sinful selves, their sinful selves will bring them ruin. But if they plant to please the Spirit, they will receive eternal life from the Spirit.

GALATIANS 6:7–8

My child,

The life you two share with one another can be compared to a garden. In the beginning a garden involves a lot of work. First the ground must be prepared. Then thought must be given to what you wish to grow. Then comes the planting, watering, weeding, and so on. And finally, the plants come up and the flowers bloom. In your life together, you prepare the ground by choosing to spend time with each other, choosing to value and trust and care for each other. You plant kind words and consideration, laughter and good times, talking and listening and sharing your hearts, your times of work, your play and rest. You water these tender plants with prayer and hope. You weed out the distractions and commitments that keep you from each other. And you wait. Then, in time, if you are faithful, tender plants will begin to push their way out of the ground. (Protect them well, for they will wither in the face of harshness or neglect.) Soon buds will appear and open, and your garden of love will be in bloom. But know this, my child: You cannot plant onions and expect roses to come up. If you plant selfishness and criticism, your garden will not be a thing of beauty. What you put in is what will come up. So honor each other and me by planting grace and tenderness and charity.

Then watch love bloom,
God

Learn What Love Is Not

Love is not jealous, it does not brag, and it is not proud.

1 Corinthians 13:4b

Dearest child,

Sometimes you can learn what something is by looking closely at what it is not. Love is not jealous, it does not brag, and it is not proud. Look closely now and you will see why these qualities cannot be part of love. Jealousy, bragging, and pride seek only to aggrandize the self, whereas love seeks to lift up the loved one. Those who are proud take all the credit for their own success and revel in it. Braggarts begin every sentence with the pronoun "I." They can barely listen to what someone else is saying because they're already busy mentally planning their own responses. Jealous people commit mental murder by hating the gifts and achievements of others. They operate from a stance of lack that says, "There is only so much to go around— so much love, talent, beauty, approval. If someone else has an abundance of these things, that person is keeping some from me. If I can tear down these things in that person's life, I can have more of them for myself." The only cure for the proud, the boastful, the jealous is to confess these attitudes as sin, receive my forgiveness, and be continually filled with the perfect love of Jesus. For only the heart that is continually being filled with love can allow that love to overflow into the lives of others. Come to me daily, my child.

Be filled to overflowing,
God

Be Rich in Love

*It is better to eat vegetables with those who love you
than to eat meat with those who hate you.*

PROVERBS 15:17

Child of mine,

I wish for you a good life, rich in the things that matter most. And what is the most important ingredient of a good life? Is it wealth? Many people act as though it is. But I tell you this: Love matters far more than money. For you can earn small wages and live in a humble home, but if there is love within your walls, you are rich indeed! You can make a humble pot of potato soup for supper and serve it on the kitchen table, but if love sits down to dine with you, your meal will be a feast! It is easy to look at the outer trappings of a wealthy person's life and jump to the conclusion he or she "has it all." But the truth is, all the wealth in the world cannot buy life's most priceless treasure—love. And without love, people endure the worst kind of poverty no matter how much money they have. So as you evaluate your own life, my child, don't measure your riches in dollars and cents. Look at the love you can give and receive, and you'll understand the real value of your existence.

Be rich in love!
God

Trust That I Am at Work

If a Christian man has a wife who is not a believer, and she is happy to live with him, he must not divorce her. And if a Christian woman has a husband who is not a believer, and he is happy to live with her, she must not divorce him.

Wife, you don't know; maybe you will save your husband. And husband, you don't know; maybe you will save your wife.

1 CORINTHIANS 7:12–13, 16

My dear child,

*I*f your loved one does not believe in me or follow me, I know you are living in a difficult place. You long for shared beliefs. You yearn to open your whole heart to your mate, but you don't have that freedom. You see other couples who have found the joy of spiritual oneness, and you don't understand why it could not be so for you. You have prayed and prayed and waited and wished. I see your struggle, my child. You are not alone in it. I am with you. I want these things for you in your marriage even more than you do. But I am asking you to trust me to work in my time and my season. Do not force your hand. You cannot nag or argue or browbeat another person into accepting your beliefs, however strong or logical your arguments may seem to you. I created each of you with a free will so that you could each have the freedom to choose me on your own. Don't try to take this freedom of choice away from your mate. Can you simply love that dear one for me today, demonstrating the beauty of a heart that is filled with me? Can you laugh and find joy in the daily things? Can you pray, believe, and trust my Spirit to work in your loved one's life? Don't give up.

I am at work!
God

Value Love Above Everything

I may have the gift of prophecy. I may understand all the secret things of God and have all knowledge, and I may have faith so great I can move mountains. But even with all these things, if I do not have love, then I am nothing.

1 CORINTHIANS 13:2

All these commands and all others are really only one rule: Love your neighbor as you love yourself. Love never hurts a neighbor, so loving is obeying all the law.

ROMANS 13:9b–10

My child,

*The most gifted people are not necessarily the ones who most resemble my Son, Jesus, though he was indeed gifted. But the true hallmark of his character was his pure and abiding love. For above every other wonderful thing he was, Jesus was first and foremost a container of my love who walked out my loving will in his daily circumstances. That is why to walk as a Christian (a Christ-one) is to be remade into a love-container, a vessel filled with his Spirit of love. Don't you see? Your giftedness counts for little if you don't know how to love. But once you are operating on Spirit power, love will be at the root of all you do! It will be your motivation and your **modus operandi**. It will fuel your gifts and empower your faith in the One whose name is Love. So, my child, value love above everything, and allow my Holy Spirit of love to fill and fuel your heart to live as a disciple of my loving Son.*

Your Father and his,
God

Words Are Packages of Power

How beautiful is the person
    who comes over the mountains to bring good news,
who announces peace
    and brings good news. . . .

                  Isaiah 52:7a

    Pleasant words are like a honeycomb,
        making people happy and healthy.

               Proverbs 16:24

    Starting a quarrel is like a leak in a dam,
        so stop it before a fight breaks out.

               Proverbs 17:14

The right word spoken at the right time
    is as beautiful as gold apples in a silver bowl.

               Proverbs 25:11

My dear child,

*I*f only you knew how important your words are! They are potent little packages of power with a capacity to do great good or great harm. With them you can bless or curse, build up or tear down, wound or heal. Just as the body can be destroyed with a gun or a knife, the human spirit can be destroyed by harsh and wounding words. Just as an interior decorator can create a warm and gracious physical environment with the colors he or she chooses, you can create a warm and welcoming spiritual environment by the words you choose. Knowing that you have this kind of power on the tip of your tongue, be cautious, my child. Choose your words carefully and prayerfully. Make a prayerful decision in my presence each morning to decorate the day ahead of you with gentle, caring words. If you let me, I will help you find specific words of blessing and encouragement to speak to the ones you love. Bring the good news of my mercy into the atmosphere of your home, and watch the lights come on!

Use words wisely,
God

Let My Spirit Make You "One"

> . . . Make me very happy by having the same thoughts, sharing the same love, and having one mind and purpose.

PHILIPPIANS 2:2

> Since you are God's children, God sent the Spirit of his Son into your hearts.

GALATIANS 4:6

My own dear child,

*I*s there a gulf between you and your loved one today? Are you feeling more separated than connected, more distance than closeness, more "twoness" than "oneness"? Don't despair, my child. I know Someone who is in the business of making two into one. It is his specialty! When two people trust Jesus and invite him into the midst of their hearts and their marriage, he brings with him my Holy Spirit, and immediately the Spirit gets to work. He begins tearing down partitions that separate and building connectors. He begins softening hearts that have hardened and opening emotional doors that have been closed. When my Son and my Spirit move into your heart, they open your life to the power of my love, my mercy, my forgiveness, my vision, my light, and my reconciliation. And when Jesus dwells in the quiet center of your heart, you can talk to him in prayer and gain his counsel. You can share your needs and receive his help. You can place every conversation and decision and interaction in your marriage under his merciful covering. And you can learn to walk the road he carves out for you—the road that can lead two hearts, at last, to be one.

Seek my Son and welcome my Spirit,
God

Live Out of "The Center"

In your lives you must think and act like Christ Jesus.

PHILIPPIANS 2:5

I was put to death on the cross with Christ, and I do not live anymore—it is Christ who lives in me. I still live in my body, but I live by faith in the Son of God who loved me and gave himself to save me.

GALATIANS 2:20

Dear child,

What makes some love relationships turn sour? It's not all that hard to understand. Living day in and day out with the same person through all kinds of stressful situations makes it easy, at times, to slide into conversation and behavior that displays more impatience, disrespect, and anger than love. That's "only human," some might say. What do people mean when they use that expression? I wonder. Could they mean that you're going to fall short sooner or later anyway, so you might as well give up trying and drop to the lowest common denominator of human behavior? Well, I want more for you than that. Because you have asked me into your heart, you don't have to be "only human." You can be a human container filled with the divine Spirit of love—the Holy Spirit of Jesus Christ. And as you learn to live out of that deep, peace-filled center of your life, you will find yourself more and more able to choose to act and react as Jesus would, with graciousness and faithfulness and love. And as you continue choosing at each small crossroads to yield to the Spirit, you'll find that the love in your heart will flourish.

You're more than "only human!"
God

It's Time to Go On!

The Lord says, "Forget what happened before,
    and do not think about the past.
Look at the new thing I am going to do.
    It is already happening. Don't you see it?"

ISAIAH 43:18–19

Don't ask, "Why was life better in the 'good old days'?"
    It is not wise to ask such questions.

ECCLESIASTES 7:10

Dear child of mine,

A *marriage is a living, growing, changing thing. There will be many different seasons in this married life you share with one another. All are valuable, and all can be turned to good. In every season there will be things to enjoy, challenges to rise to, and changes to accept. It is very counterproductive to keep clutching at the way things used to be, constantly looking over your shoulder at some season that is now past. You must learn to let go and go on. As I lead and guide you through every step of your life together, keep your eyes open to see and accept the new thing I am doing in your midst. Keep your heart tender to accept the new season to which I am leading you. If you are willing to go on, you will find in each new season some precious moments, some unexpected treasures. This you can be sure of. So don't look back my child.*

It's time to go on!
God

He Still Works Miracles!

Two days later there was a wedding in the town of Cana in Galilee. . . . When all the wine was gone, Jesus' mother said to him, "They have no more wine." . . . Jesus said to the servants, "Fill the jars with water." So they filled the jars to the top. Then he said to them, "Now take some out and give it to the master of the feast." So they took the water to the master. When he tasted it, the water had become wine.

JOHN 2:1, 3, 7–9a

Dearest child,

*I*sn't it interesting that my Son's very first miracle was performed at a wedding? Do you realize that Jesus is still doing miracles in the lives of married people today? Often in a marriage trials and trouble take their toll, and a man and woman, once so much in love, look wearily at their relationship only to find that the sparkle has gone out of it. Just as the wine at the wedding feast in Cana was depleted, the excitement and the romance seem to have run dry. My child, if that time comes in your marriage, don't be surprised and don't despair. For in the same way that my Son touched the flavorless, colorless water and turned it into the sparkling, delicious, deep red drink of a celebration, so can he touch your two hearts, restoring the color and excitement of your love. Turn to him, my children. And like the servants at the wedding feast, be obedient to whatever instructions he whispers in your hearts. Allow him to touch you, rekindle your commitment, and work a miracle in your relationship.

Believe me, he can do it!
God

Angry Words Can Cause Damage

My dear brothers and sisters, always be willing to listen and slow to speak. Do not become angry easily, because anger will not help you live the right kind of life God wants. So put out of your life every evil thing and every kind of wrong. Then in gentleness accept God's teaching that is planted in your hearts, which can save you.

JAMES 1:19–21

*Someone with a quick temper does foolish things,
but someone with understanding remains calm.*

PROVERBS 14:17

My child,

*O*h, if only you knew the damage rash, angry words can cause. Listen to me now. I tell you this because I love you, and it breaks my heart when I see one of my children throwing away a chance for happiness. Believe me, I know that marriage is not always easy. Many days it can feel like walking a tightrope: There's only one way to stay on the wire and so many chances to fall flat on your face! But one sure strategy for staying on course is to learn to wait before lashing out. Learn to listen— really listen. There is always another side to the story. I'm not telling you to bundle up your feelings of frustration and stuff them away in the basement of your soul. You'll end up with a very crowded basement if you do that! But learn to go slowly, hear the other side, pray for wisdom, and then speak your feelings without casting blame or shame, without blowing up and saying things you cannot take back. Remember that apologies are wonderful things, but they can get pretty threadbare if your reckless temper gives you cause to overuse them. Better to bite your tongue and hold your temper! What I'm teaching you now can make or break your marriage.

Take it from me!
God

Keep Love Alive

It is hard to find a good wife,
because she is worth more than rubies.
She does him good and not harm
for as long as she lives.

PROVERBS 31:10, 12

My own dear child,

Very often, love simply means using your common sense. There is nothing very mysterious about it. It means doing good and not harm. How can you "do good" in your relationship? By being open and honest with your loved one—talking things out, listening with compassion, sharing your own feelings. By desiring the best for your partner, just as strongly as you desire it for yourself, and by putting loving actions behind those desires. That's about as simple a recipe for marital happiness as anyone could ask. But just because it's simply stated doesn't mean it's easy to do. Why do you see so many marriages around you failing? It is almost always because at some point in the marriage, someone has stopped "doing good." Someone has stopped desiring the best for the other person and started selfishly focusing on self only. Someone has stopped openly sharing heartfelt feelings and started selfishly guarding his or her heart. Like persistent little streams can, in time, erode the face of a mountain, persistent selfishness can erode the face of love itself. So use your common sense! Unselfishly reach out and do good things for your mate, and you'll be keeping love alive!

Devotedly,
God

Throw Open the Doors of Your Heart

Open your homes to each other, without complaining. Each of you has received a gift to use to serve others. Be good servants of God's various gifts of grace.

1 Peter 4:9–10

Then the King will answer, "I tell you the truth, anything you did for even the least of my people here, you also did for me."

Matthew 25:40

My dear child,

*D*o you have four walls, a roof, and a front door where guests may enter? Never for a minute take this for granted. In a world where many are homeless and hungry, abandoned and cast out, a home is a precious treasure. It can be a castle or a cabin, an elaborate townhouse or a tiny apartment. However large or small, however elegant or plain, if you call it home, it is a gift. And if those within your walls love one another and love me, your home can be a tiny outpost of heaven in the midst of a reckless world. It can be an island of caring in a sea of hostility. Make your guestlist prayerfully. Include some who can minister and some who need ministry. Lovingly "prepare a place." Then throw open the doors of your heart and welcome each one as you would welcome me. And when your guests are gathered and gladly taken in, stand back, my child, and watch me work. Watch your home become a place where hearts are healed!

> I will do it,
> God

You Were Designed for Love

You made [human beings] a little lower than the angels
and crowned them with glory and honor.

PSALM 8:5

LORD you do everything for me.
LORD, your love continues forever.
Do not leave us, whom you made.

PSALM 138:8

Even when your hair has turned gray,
I will take care of you.
I made you and will take care of you.
I will carry you and save you.

ISAIAH 46:4

My dear child,

You were made in my image, created in my likeness, crowned with glory and honor, fashioned and intended to live in love. You were designed to receive my love and to give it to others as I have given it to you. What is the hallmark of my love? It is my faithfulness. My love is not capricious nor fickle nor haphazard. I entered into my covenant with you for life, **forever**. My love is constant and dependable. It will be the same in a thousand years as it is today, the same as it was from before the earth's foundations were laid. I loved you when I formed you in your mother's womb. I loved you as a sweet, innocent child. I love you now, right where you are, regardless of where you have been or what you have done. And when you are old and your hair is gray, will I love you or care for you less? Of course not! So now I ask, **Can you love like this in your marriage?** Oh, my child, let me fill you with my faithful love so that you too can love faithfully.

Today and forever,
God

Love Is a Quiet Miracle

I may give away everything I have, and I may even give my body as an offering to be burned. But I gain nothing if I do not have love.

1 Corinthians 13:3

My dear child,

*P*lease be very clear about this—I am not asking you to rush out and do something extremely dramatic or outlandishly heroic. I'm not asking for a great outward show that might impress the thrill-seeking world, for there is nothing worthy to be gained in that. I am asking, instead, for the quiet, inner conversion of your heart that will turn you from a self-seeker into a God-seeker, from a self-lover into an other-lover. The heart conversion I speak of may not make the headlines or amaze the general public. But it is the kind of quiet miracle that will, quite simply, revolutionize your whole life and thereby touch and change the small corner of the world in which you live. And strangely enough, once your heart has been turned inside out by love, you may find yourself capable of doing great things without even needing or feeding on the attention they may bring.

Come. Learn to love,
God

Hold Your Possessions Lightly

The Lord owns the world and everything in it.
DEUTERONOMY 10:14

You put [human beings] in charge of everything you made.
You put all things under their control.
PSALM 8:6

I was naked when I was born,
and I will be naked when I die.
The Lord gave these things to me,
and he has taken them away.
Praise the name of the Lord.
JOB 1:21

Those who are trusted with something valuable must show they are worthy of that trust.
1 CORINTHIANS 4:2

Remember the words Jesus said: "It is more blessed to give than to receive."
ACTS 20:35

You must not steal. You must not cheat people, and you must not lie to each other.
LEVITICUS 19:11

My God will use his wonderful riches in Christ Jesus to give you everything you need.
PHILIPPIANS 4:19

My precious children,

When you are out in the beauty of my creation, does it ever occur to you that I am the owner of all you see? I have put human beings in charge during their temporary stay in this world, but I am still the Owner. Whatever you own is mine, on loan to you for a season—your money, your home, your car, your clothes, and your other possessions. When death separates you from this earthly life, it will also separate you from these things. If you can understand and accept this fact, it will help you to hold these things lightly and be good stewards. Find out what my Word says about handling money. Come to me with your financial decisions, and seek my guidance. Prayerfully design a spending plan and stay with it. Deal honestly with all people in all matters. Give generously to those in need. And trust me to supply all that you require.

Your Provider,
God

Honor the One You Love

Give each other more honor than you want for yourselves.

ROMANS 12:10b

When you do things, do not let selfishness or pride be your guide. Instead, be humble and give more honor to others than to yourselves.

PHILIPPIANS 2:3

Do to others what you want them to do to you.

MATTHEW 7:12

My child,

Everyone likes to feel important. Everyone enjoys being complimented and treated well. But nothing strains a loving relationship more than when both people are constantly tending their own pride and safeguarding their own rights by competing for the compliments and pushing for the place of honor. Let me lift you above the scrambling and the competition by sharing a secret with you. There is tremendous joy in giving honor to the one you love instead of always seeking it for yourself. Find that joy today by thinking of some small, heartfelt way of showing extra respect—some way of demonstrating your care and concern. But be careful not to use flattery or manipulation. That's as bad as lying, and most people can see right through it. Instead, be sincere. Think of how good you would feel if you were treated with a little extra kindness. Then choose to show that same kind of treatment to the one you love. You won't regret it!

Your Father,
God

Come and Be Filled!

I pray that Christ will live in your hearts by faith and that your life will be strong in love and be built on love. And I pray that you and all God's holy people will have the power to understand the greatness of Christ's love—how wide and how long and how high and how deep that love is. Christ's love is greater than anyone can ever know, but I pray that you will be able to know that love. Then you can be filled with the fullness of God.

EPHESIANS 3:17–19

I pray that the God who gives hope will fill you with much joy and peace while you trust in him. Then your hope will overflow by the power of the Holy Spirit.

ROMANS 15:13

Child of mine,

*Here is an incredible clue to the mystery of love. The very best way to live a life of love on earth is to be centered in a deep and powerful heavenly love. When you are centered in the love of my Son, **you** can begin to grow in **him**. And when you invite him to dwell in the center of who you are, **he** can begin to grow in **you**. You'll find that once the Spirit of Jesus is at home in your heart, your eyes will be opened to the immensity of his love. There is no map big enough to measure his compassion and caring for you. It reaches up far higher than the planets in their orbits. It reaches down far deeper than the caves beneath the sea. Its boundaries are flung out to span the width of many worlds. And the length of its endurance stretches to the farthest corners of forever. When your heart is continually filled to all fullness with his love like a pitcher that is continually filled with water, there will be an overflow! And all who come close to you will be touched and warmed and healed and welcomed by his love, which fills your heart. So . . .*

> *Come and be filled!*
> *God*

Desire Peace and Pursue It

Do all you can to live a peaceful life. Take care of your own business, and do your own work as we have already told you.

1 Thessalonians 4:11

That fairness will bring peace,
and it will bring calm and safety forever.

Isaiah 32:17

Those who work to bring peace are happy,
because God will call them his children.

Matthew 5:9

Dear child of mine,

Though you live in a world of conflict and confusion, I would not have you follow suit. For you are not to live as citizens of this world but of another kingdom—a peaceful kingdom in which love is the law and peace is the standard. One of the surest ways to secure peace is to do what you know is right, taking care of things as they arise and not putting them off until a later time. Doing what you know is right brings a quiet, calm sense of confidence into your inner life that spills over into your home and your relationships. You honor me when you live like this, for when others see the peace in your home and family life, they may want what you have. Then you can lead them to me, and there will be that many more peaceful hearts in this world of conflict!

Desire peace and pursue it,
God

Speak Kindness and Show Mercy

Be kind and loving to each other, and forgive each other just as God forgave you in Christ.

Ephesians 4:32

Those who show mercy to others are happy,
because God will show mercy to them.

Matthew 5:7

Dear child,

*K*indness is like a lovely flower whose fragrance is lifted and carried on a breeze so that all nearby are touched by its loveliness. Kindness inspires kindness, setting off a chain reaction in hearts and carrying its blessing from person to person. Speak gentle, caring words to your loved ones first thing in the morning, and you will set off a chain of loving behavior that will touch the people they encounter all day long.

Acts of mercy are like sips of cool water to the thirsty spirit. They refresh those who are weary, restoring energy and hope. Do you realize how many people in this world are "dying of thirst"? As you quench the daily thirst for mercy in the lives of your loved ones, your home will become an oasis in a desert landscape. So remember these two things, my child . . .

Speak kindness and show mercy,
God

Discover the Meaning of Oneness

Does your life in Christ give you strength? Does his love comfort you? Do we share together in the spirit? Do you have mercy and kindness? If so, make me very happy by having the same thoughts, sharing the same love, and having one mind and purpose.

PHILIPPIANS 2:1–2

Holy Father, keep them safe by the power of your name, the name you gave me, so that they will be one, just as you and I are one.

JOHN 17:11

My child,

Your spiritual life is like a pantry that has been loaded with good things. On the shelves of your pantry are all the qualities of my own Son's flawless character: his strength and comfort, his mercy and kindness. Why has he supplied you so well with this storehouse of spiritual blessings? He knows that as you strive to live in love, you will need more strength of character than you naturally possess. So he has given you access, through the Holy Spirit, to his own character! If you will learn to reach into your spiritual pantry for those Christ-supplied qualities, they will enable you to have unity of mind and heart and spirit with your marriage partner. Learning to access the character of Christ in yourself will enable you to care, comfort, and encourage each other in ways you never could before. You will understand what Jesus meant by "oneness," and you'll find ways of bringing that oneness into your loving relationship. For never are two people more at one with each other than when each of them is at one with Christ.

Enter into this mystery,
God

Don't Play the World's Game

Wait and trust the LORD.
Don't be upset when others get rich
or when someone else's plans succeed.

PSALM 37:7

I am not telling you this because I need anything. I have learned to be satisfied with the things I have and with everything that happens. I know how to live when I am poor, and I know how to live when I have plenty. I have learned the secret of being happy at any time in everything that happens, when I have enough to eat and when I go hungry, when I have more than I need and when I do not have enough. I can do all things through Christ, because he gives me strength.

PHILIPPIANS 4:11–13

My precious child,

*The world invites you to compete in a mad scramble for more—more possessions, more money, more power, more prestige, more trophies of success. The world measures personal worth by the numbers in your bankbook and the kind of automobile you drive. This materialistic mentality is very seductive. It calls to you from magazine ads; it beckons to you from storeroom displays, TV commercials, and perhaps even from the lifestyle of the neighbors next door. But hear me, my child. You and your family need not be defined by the world. I encourage you to withdraw from that race. Drop out of the competition. Don't play the world's game for another second! You are a priceless treasure, not because of what you earn or own, but because I created you and Jesus died for you. You need not compete for **my** affection. My kingdom does not grade on the curve. There is a place for you in my heart that no one else can take away. So find your contentment in my love and provision. Get your identity from me and your strength from my Son.*

Devotedly,
God

Learn to Love As You Were Designed To

The holy women who lived long ago and followed God made themselves beautiful, yielding to their own husbands. Sarah obeyed Abraham, her husband, and called him her master. And you women are true children of Sarah if you always do what is right and are not afraid.

In the same way, you husbands should live with your wives in an understanding way, since they are weaker than you. But show them respect, because God gives them the same blessing he gives you—the grace that gives true life. Do this so that nothing will stop your prayers.

1 PETER 3:5, 7

My children,

If it were a perfect world, I would not have to be writing you this letter. You would already know how to relate to each other perfectly. You would fit together flawlessly in my plan for marital harmony. Wives would yield to and honor their husbands, and husbands would respect, honor, and understand their wives. But I'm sure you realize that the world you live in is far from perfect. It is tainted by twisted ideas of right and wrong. That's why there are so many women and men (even in marriages) at war with each other, distrusting each other, and living out a bitter hostility toward each other. Oh, my children, you need not live like this. Draw near to me, and I will help you understand my perfect plan for you. It is a plan that brings honor and fulfillment to both of you. It is a plan with order and spiritual symmetry built into it so that you can live and love together in peace and joy. Trust my mercy. Read my Word and digest its meaning. And learn to love as you were designed to.

Your Creator and Father,
God

Make Up Before Tomorrow

When you are angry, do not sin, and be sure to stop being angry before the end of the day.

Do not be bitter or angry or mad. Never shout angrily or say things to hurt others. Never do anything evil.

EPHESIANS 4:26, 31

Those who do not control themselves
are like a city whose walls are broken down.

PROVERBS 25:28

My dear child,

*P*artners in a healthy love relationship should be able to experience, share, and deal with all kinds of emotions, both positive and negative. But anger is a negative emotion that is certain to cause trouble in a relationship if it is not handled wisely. The wisest way to handle anger is to confess it and release it to me. For if you hold on to it and nurse it and allow it to fester, anger can become bitterness, bitterness can become hatred, and hatred is poison to the spirit. So when you detect anger in your heart, above all, don't act on it! Stop right where you are and confess it to me. Don't allow your anger to carry over from one day to the next. Don't give it an overnight foothold in your heart. Forgive one another and be reconciled before the day is over.

Make up before tomorrow!
God

Acceptance Is a Loving Thing

Love patiently accepts all things.
1 Corinthians 13:7a

Let your patience show itself perfectly in what you do.
James 1:4a

My child,

*L*iving together in love is difficult for everyone who tries it. Conflicts and disagreements are part of life. For this reason, one of the most loving things you can learn to do is to accept some imperfections in the ones you love. And also, accept the fact that not everything in every situation is going to go the way you want it to, even if you feel certain your way is best. Don't think for a minute that this kind of acceptance is weak-willed or wishy-washy. Don't think I'm asking you to compromise my truth or sell out your ideals. No way! What I **am** asking you to do is to accept your loved ones even though they're still in the process of being made whole. Accept them even though they're not yet perfect, remembering that this is exactly how I accept you. I'm also asking you to take little inconveniences in your stride, without losing your gentle spirit—to deal with life's petty irritations without losing your sense of humor. Oh, my child, as you live in love, let me help you develop patience.

You won't regret it,
God

Let Me Be Your Guide

*If you go the wrong way—to the right or to the left—you will hear a voice
behind you saying, "This is the right way. You should go this way."*

ISAIAH 30:21

Dear child,

*L*oving for a lifetime is like taking a long, long journey, so don't expect to arrive the very first day! Every morning on this journey of love you set out to go another mile. Some days are sunny; the road is smooth, and your hopes are high. On days like that, you make definite progress! But on other days the clouds cover the sun, and the road is full of rocks and bumps, and you can't seem to get out of your own way. Or you try a shortcut that ends up being a "long cut," and you find you've actually backtracked and lost days or weeks in the bargain. It's so easy to get discouraged at times like that. It's tempting to start thinking about turning back or just plain quitting. Don't give up! Don't turn back! Instead, turn to me. I want to guide you on your journey. Come to me each morning before you set out. Talk to me about your travel plans. Spread out your map before me, and we'll look at it together. I'll help you chart your course. And when you put your foot in the road and begin, I'll be right there with you, saying, "Take a right," or "Turn left here at the corner." You can trust me to help you stay on track and enjoy the journey.

Let me be your guide,
God

Love Is the Binding Force

. . . *Always do these things: Show mercy to others, be kind, humble, gentle, and patient. Get along with each other, and forgive each other. If someone does wrong to you, forgive that person because the Lord forgave you. Do all these things; but most important, love each other. Love is what holds you all together in perfect unity.*

COLOSSIANS 3:12b–14

My dear child,

*U*nless there is a binding force, separate things will not hold together. The binding force of glue seals many separate pages into a book. The binding forces of nails, screws, putty, and cement hold a house together and make it strong. Magnetic fields create a binding force for metals. Gravity is the binding force that holds your body to the earth's surface. But in human relationships love is the binding force. As you learn to love, kindness and gentleness and patience will bind heart to heart. Mercy, like a magnetic field, will draw two lives into unity; and forgiveness, like gravity, keeps a marriage grounded and down to earth. So do not fear the power of the world to separate you and your loved one, my child, but let me train you in the school of love. And love will be the binding force that brings unity.

Live in love,
God

This World Is Not Your Final Destination

Our knowledge and our ability to prophesy are not perfect. But when perfection comes, the things that are not perfect will end.

1 CORINTHIANS 13:9–10

Listen! I am coming soon! . . . I am the Alpha and the Omega, the First and the Last, the Beginning and the End.

Happy are those who wash their robes so that they will receive the right to eat the fruit from the tree of life and may go through the gates into the city.

REVELATION 22:12–14

Dearest child,

*S*omething within you yearns for a perfect love, a perfect romance, a perfect marriage. You know all too well that you live on an imperfect planet inhabited by imperfect people, and yet you cannot seem to quiet that yearning deep within for something more. Don't you realize that I placed that yearning in your heart when I designed you? You were designed to walk through a green garden with a good God in perfect love. And that ache at the core of who you are is really an unconscious memory woven into the fiber of your being—an unconscious reaching back to that now unreachable realm I once called Eden. Eden, where, for a moment in time, love was lovely and pure . . . and perfect. But don't worry, my child. This world is not forever. It is not your final destination. For as you move through this life with me, you are moving toward a place where all your tears will be dried and all your yearning, fulfilled. So bring your whole heart into your love on this planet, reaching for the best, all the while forgiving others and yourself when human love falls short. For you can content yourself with the certainty that you are destined for an everlasting love that is perfection itself!

Eternally yours,
God

Hold On to Love

[Love] always trusts, always hopes, and always remains strong.
Love never ends.

1 Corinthians 13:7b–8a

Your love must be real. Hate what is evil, and hold on to what is good. . . . Be
joyful because you have hope. Be patient when trouble comes, and pray at all times.

Romans 12:9, 12

My children,

May your love for each other be courageous. May it span the seasons of the soul. May it flow through the ups and downs of your life together like a small stream that flows as steadily through level pastures as through rocky ground. And as things change, may your love deepen to the depth of those changes. May it carve a channel through the bedrock of your problems like a stream carves a channel through which its waters flow. Over all the years of challenges and changes, may your courage and commitment persevere. May your passion pour itself out more and more until that stream becomes a river, and the channel that it flows through is deep and sure and wide. Hold on to each other, my children, and hold on to love. For it is a mercy and a treasure, and to let it go would be a grievous loss.

Everlastingly!
God